The Adventures of Bones, The Big Black Dog

"Bones needs a playmate"

He was a sweet dog, and though very large, he loved all the animals in the neighborhood and all the animals at the park and all the animals of the forest. He especially loved children but he could not find an animal to play with?

At a nearby park he met Josiah's and Callie's pet chicken Cluck. It was Bones first chicken he had ever had seen and all he wanted to do was play! But the chicken was scared and said, "I will not play with you", you will hurt me and chickens do not play with dogs! So Bones left to try and find another animal he could play with...

A short while later at a nearby park he found a herd of cows and he said, "oh boy they are about my size surely they will want to play with me!"

And he tried and tried to get them to play
they wanted nothing to do with him and
Bones was beginning to wonder if any animal
would ever play with him?

And Bones started getting very sad and that was not like Bones, Why would no other animal would play with him? What did he do? Was he too big? "why does not any other animal like me?"

And then one day his owner heard of a
special place where there were many
friendly dogs and some might want to play.
"The dog park", and Bones was told that he
would soon be going to the dog park and he
got very Happy!"Can we go now! Can we go
now!"

The first dog Bones met was "Max", an airdale, and Max was happy to see Bones. And Bones was VERY HAPPY to see Max!....."Max will you play with me?" And Max said, "Of course!"

The next thing you know they started
playing......

Then they started wrestling and Bones was
very Happy and Max became his best friend.

And when they where done Max said, "See you later Bones!", "Make sure you come back and play tomorrow!"

The next Dog Bones found at the dog park was Roxie, a doberman pincher, and Bones asked Roxie, "Can you play? And Roxie said, "Sure" and they too started to play.

After they played they decided to go on a walk down a trail to the creek where the continued to play and swim

And Bones went to yet another the dog park
and found another playmate Cody, a
labrador, and Bones asked Cody "will you
play with me?" and Cody said, "Anytime!"
and they played and played.

And later that evening Bones was very tired
and very happy as he realized there where
many animals he could play with and he
slept very deeply and dreamed many things
and he also found out that not all animals
can be playmates and you must seek out your
friends.

This book is dedicated to Motoko Chiba and her amazing spirit

It is also dedicated to all the great dogs in the world that touch our lives daily with their unconditional love

Bones is of course an actual dog that lives in Boise, Idaho. He is half mastiff and half Newfoundland and is an AKC registered therapy dog and does water rescue without training. At 4 months old he weighed 64 pounds, at 6 months old he hit 95 pounds, and at 10 months old he weighed 132 pounds. I could go to work come home 8 hours later and you could tell he grew! At 4 months old if you were sick he would lick your hand and still does it to this day. At 14 months old he could pop a full size basketball in his mouth. Now at almost 2 ½ years old he still chases his tail and is a "laser" dog. He can get any dog to play and three strangers told me their dogs would not play with any dog but Bones.

Edited by Callie & Josiah

Special thanks to Katie Rosenburg who took Bones in,

(And loves him like her own), in my time of need.

I would also like to thank John Grogan, (Marley & Me); Jon Katz, (A Dog Year: Twelve Months, Fours Dogs and Me); And Susanne Charleson (Scent of the Missing); Ace Collins (Man's Best Friend). All four books I read in about a month and somewhere during the middle they inspired me to write about Bones.

I would also like to thank Bones who without him none of this would be possible. I looked for 2 years for him and at 53 I never got to pick out a dog until Bones. He has the ability to bring out the best in every animal and person he meets.

And I would like to thank our heavenly Father who continues to astound me with each passing day and each passing moment.

Made in the USA
Middletown, DE
14 March 2019